TIME FOR KIDS

I Can

Dona Herweck Rice

Consultant

Timothy Rasinski, Ph.D
Kent State University

Publishing Credits

Dona Herweck Rice, *Editor-in-Chief*
Lee Aucoin, *Creative Director*
Conni Medina, M.A.Ed., *Editorial Director*
Jamey Acosta, *Editor*
Robin Erickson, *Designer*
Stephanie Reid, *Photo Editor*
Rachelle Cracchiolo, M.S.Ed., *Publisher*

Image Credits
Cover Comstock Images/Getty Images;
p.3 Arthus Tilley; Jade Albert Studio, Inc./Getty Images;
p.4 Don Smetzer/Getty Images; p.5 Lucian Coman /Shutterstock;
p.6 jpmediainc/istockophoto; p.7 Andresr/Shutterstock; p.8 akajeff/istockphoto;
p.9 Photo Library; p.10 BaileyOne/Shutterstock; p.11 Discover/Dreamstime;
back cover Andresr/Shutterstock

Based on writing from *TIME For Kids.*

Teacher Created Materials
5301 Oceanus Drive
Huntington Beach, CA 92649-1030
http://www.tcmpub.com

ISBN 978-1-4333-3569-3

Printed by: 51497
Printed in: Taiwan

I can!

I can play.

I can dig.

I can swing.

I can run.

I can write.

I can read.

I can love.

I can! I can!
I can do it.

Words to Know

can
dig
do
I
it
love
play
read
run
swing
write